WORKING DOGS

by Josh Gregory

Children's Press®

An Imprint of Scholastic Inc.
New York   Toronto   London   Auckland   Sydney
Mexico City   New Delhi   Hong Kong
Danbury, Connecticut

Content Consultant
Dr. Stephen S. Ditchkoff
Professor of Wildlife Sciences
Auburn University
Auburn, Alabama

Photographs 2013: Alamy Images/Juniors Bildarchiv GmbH/F318:
20, 23; AP Images/Paul Sakuma: 15; Bob Italiano: 44 foreground, 45
foreground; Corbis Images/Doug Pearson/JAI: cover; Dreamstime: 28
(Elisabeth Hammerschmid), 44 background, 45 background (Monkie),
1, 46 (Risto40); Europics: 4, 5 background, 16; Getty Images: 27
(Jeffrey L. Jaquish, ZingPix.com), 32 (Justin Sullivan), 12 (Stan Honda/
AFP), 5 top, 8 (Vedros & Associates); K9 Storm Incorporated: 2, 3;
Media Bakery: 5 bottom, 40 (JI), 36 (Steve Smith); Reuters/Mike
Stone: 39; REX USA/Craig Borrow/Newspix: 11; Shutterstock, Inc.:
31 (Kachalkina Veronika), 7 (Marcel Jancovic), 19 (Oleg Kozlov); The
Image Works: 35 (J. Wildgruber/SZ Photo), 24 (Sally Fear/Impact/
HIP).

Library of Congress Cataloging-in-Publication Data
Gregory, Josh.
  Working dogs / by Josh Gregory.
      pages cm.—(Nature's children)
  Includes bibliographical references and index.
  Audience: Ages 9–12.
  Audience: Grades 4–6.
  ISBN 978-0-531-20984-4 (lib. bdg.)
  ISBN 978-0-531-24310-7 (pbk.)
  1. Working dogs—Juvenile literature. I. Title.
  SF428.2.G745 2013
  636.73—dc23   2012034334

All rights reserved. Published in 2013
by Children's Press, an imprint of Scholastic Inc.

Printed in China 62
SCHOLASTIC, CHILDREN'S PRESS, and associated logos are
trademarks and/or registered trademarks of Scholastic Inc.

4 5 6 7 8 9 10 R 22 21 20 19 18 17 16

Working Dogs

Class	Mammalia
Order	Carnivora
Family	Canidae
Genus	*Canis*
Species	*Canis lupus familiaris*
World distribution	Worldwide
Habitat	Anywhere humans are found
Distinctive physical characteristics	Vary widely in size, depending on breed; most have strong, muscular legs; all are covered in fur and have pointed teeth for tearing meat
Habits	Friendly and loyal to humans; can be trained to perform a wide variety of tasks
Diet	Wild dogs are carnivorous and hunt for prey; domestic dogs are generally fed food made from a blend of meat, vegetables, and grain

WORKING DOGS

Contents

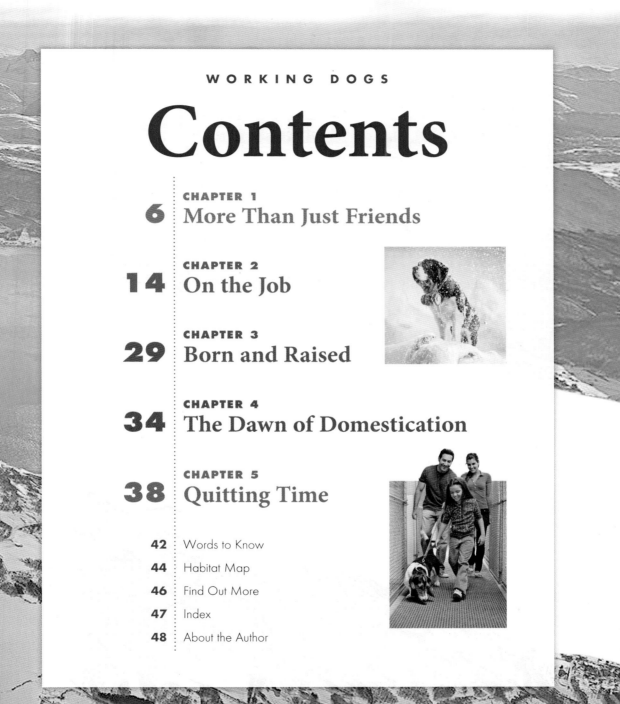

CHAPTER 1

More Than Just Friends

You have probably been around pet dogs. They are usually friendly. They like to play games, chew on toys, and be petted. Many know how to obey basic commands from their masters. Some even know a variety of impressive tricks.

Working dogs are much more than just playful companions. They are specially **bred** and trained to complete certain tasks. Their remarkable senses and physical abilities allow them to perform important jobs that would be impossible for humans to do. Only the smartest and strongest dogs are suited for most jobs. Working dogs also need to have the right personalities. Some dogs are too timid or too aggressive to work in certain fields.

If you ever see a dog out in public while it is working, be sure to leave it alone so it can do its job. Trying to pet or play with working dogs could distract them from their tasks or upset their **handlers**.

Guard dogs are trained to start and stop attacking on command.

Man's Best Friend

All working dogs are **domestic** dogs, but not all domestic dogs are working dogs. There are an estimated 600 million domestic dogs living throughout the world. Fifty million live in the United States alone. Humans have valued dogs for their loyalty and friendliness for thousands of years. Working domestic dogs are valued for their ability to perform a variety of important tasks.

Today, there are more than 400 **breeds** of domestic dogs. They vary in size. One small working breed is the Yorkshire Terrier, which can be used as a hearing dog. It weighs only 4 to 7 pounds (1.8 to 3.2 kilograms) and grows to be around 9 inches (23 centimeters) tall at the shoulder. The Saint Bernard is a larger working breed. It weighs 130 to 180 pounds (59 to 82 kg) and grows to be around 26 inches (66 cm) tall at the shoulder.

Adult Male
6 ft. (1.8 m)

Saint Bernard
26 in. (66 cm)

Yorkshire Terrier
9 in. (23 cm)

Saint Bernards are trained to rescue people who are trapped or buried in snowy areas.

Lots of Looks

All dogs share certain physical qualities. Their furry bodies, wet noses, and wagging tails are well known to any pet owner. Additionally, they all have skeletons and muscles that are built for running. Some breeds are much faster than others. But all dogs can move quickly when they need to.

All dogs are part of the same species, but every breed has a unique appearance. Some breeds have long, thick fur. Others seem to barely have any fur at all. Some have long, slender muzzles. Others have faces that are almost completely flat.

Because dogs are carnivores, their 42 teeth are shaped in a way that lets them tear through meat easily. This comes in handy for some working dogs. They can use their teeth as tools or weapons.

Some military dogs with broken teeth have them replaced with ones made of metal.

Superior Senses

Dogs have excellent senses that help them excel in a variety of jobs. A dog's most powerful sensory tool is its nose. Depending on the breed, a dog's sense of smell can be more than 1,000 times as powerful as a human's is. All dogs use this incredible sense to search for food. Working dogs are specially trained to use their sense of smell to locate other animals or humans and recognize threats.

Dogs also have excellent hearing. They can hear sounds that are much higher pitched than anything humans can hear. They can also hear sounds coming from very far away. Dogs are very good at focusing on certain kinds of sounds while ignoring other kinds. This is especially useful for dogs that assist deaf people.

A dog's vision is in some ways weaker than a human's is. Dogs are good at seeing movement, but their eyes cannot make out fine details. However, dogs can see very well in the dark. This gives them an advantage over humans at night. Dogs also have excellent **peripheral** vision because of the placement of their eyes on their heads. This helps working dogs notice everything that is going on around them.

Some dogs are trained to sniff out bedbugs in hotels, homes, and apartment buildings.

CHAPTER 2

On the Job

Law enforcement is one of the many jobs working dogs are trained for. The German Shepherd and Belgian Malinois are among the most common police dog breeds. They have the ability to find crime suspects after smelling an object that has the target's scent.

You often see these dogs at airports and other places where many people come and go. They use their powerful noses to locate hidden drugs or explosive devices where humans might not think to look.

Police dogs are called K9 officers and are important members of the police force and the community. They are sometimes buried with full police honors when killed in the line of duty.

FUN FACT!

Many breeds that excel in police work, such as Doberman pinschers and Rottweilers, also make good guard dogs.

Police dogs are at airports to search for bombs and other dangerous items.

War Dogs

Dogs that work in the military generally work in much more dangerous settings than police dogs do. Military dogs might parachute with their handlers into a war zone!

Some military dogs travel on patrols or other operations with groups of soldiers. These dogs walk ahead of the people in search of bombs, land mines, and enemies. The dogs might also enter a building before human troops to make sure it is safe. Or they might keep watch outside to prevent enemies from escaping. Military dogs also guard military bases. They help keep potential attackers from entering and search vehicles for dangerous objects, including explosive devices.

Many of these brave dogs have risked and lost their lives protecting the soldiers they work alongside. Military dogs are extremely loyal to their handlers. Some are even used in rescue missions to find and bring back wounded soldiers.

Military dogs are strapped to their handlers when parachuting out of aircraft. Some dogs must be trained to breathe through oxygen masks when they jump.

Speeding Through the Snow

Traveling through the snow on foot can be very difficult, especially if you are carrying a heavy load. Humans solved this issue hundreds of years ago by training teams of dogs to pull sleds. Many people living in snowy **climates** such as Alaska and northern Canada still use dog sleds today. The best breeds for sledding include malamutes and huskies. These dogs have thick fur to keep them warm and dry as they work. They can run a long time without getting tired and are capable of pulling heavy objects behind them. A single dog can pull a sled loaded with up to 2,000 pounds (907 kg) of weight!

Most sled dogs work together in teams. The team's handler rides behind them on the sled and yells out commands to the dogs. These commands tell the dogs how fast to go and when they should turn.

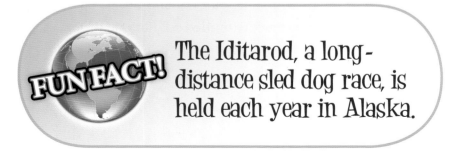

FUN FACT! The Iditarod, a long-distance sled dog race, is held each year in Alaska.

A sled dog handler develops a close relationship with his dog team.

Hunting Partners

Domestic dogs have helped humans track and retrieve **prey** for thousands of years. Long ago, humans generally relied on their own hunting abilities to survive. They eventually realized that dogs made excellent hunting partners. Even though masters usually provide their dogs with food, most domestic dogs still have many of the natural hunting **instincts** that their **ancestors** had.

Modern hunting dogs work to help humans hunt birds such as ducks, pheasants, or geese. Breeds such as setters and pointers are trained to signal when they notice prey ahead. Setters stop in their tracks and become completely still, while pointers lift one front leg. Retriever breeds are good at finding and bringing back birds that a hunter has killed.

Hunting dogs must be trained to stay back and obey their handlers. An untrained dog might react by chasing down the target animals. This would scare the animals off before the hunter had a chance to fire his gun. It would also put the dog in danger.

Retrievers sniff out the fallen birds that a hunter has shot from the sky.

Dogs to the Rescue

Search and rescue dogs are trained to work in specific situations. If a hiker is lost in the woods or a skier is buried in the snow, an air-scent rescue dog is used. These dogs have been trained to detect human scent anywhere and to go to the point where the scent is strongest. Saint Bernards and Newfoundlands, which are known for their strong swimming abilities, are trained as air-scent dogs.

Air-scent dogs are also critical in rescuing people from buildings that have collapsed because of earthquakes or bombings. These strong dogs must be able to move and climb across dangerous **terrain** while still sniffing for trapped people.

Tracking rescue dogs must follow a specific scent. They need to first smell something with the victim's scent to do their work. They are helpful at finding children who have wandered off and become lost.

Newfoundlands can rescue grown men from drowning by using a harness to pull them back to shore.

Lending a Helping Paw

Over the past several decades, dog trainers have found an important new job for man's best friend. Because people who are blind or deaf cannot sense everything that goes on around them, it helps to have an extra set of eyes or ears around. Dog breeds such as Labradors, German shepherds, and golden retrievers are perfectly suited for this task. Seeing assistance dogs guide their owners away from dangerous obstacles and help them navigate complicated areas. They let their owners know when they are near staircases and lead them safely across busy streets.

Hearing assistance dogs alert their owners to important sounds such as ringing doorbells, crying babies, and beeping fire alarms. The dogs notify their owners and lead them to the source of the noise when they hear these sounds.

Assistance dogs are allowed to go many places where other dogs are not allowed, such as to restaurants or on public transportation. Their training helps them stay calm and well behaved in loud, busy environments.

Seeing assistance dogs are sometimes called guide dogs.

Keeping the Herd in Check

Common farm animals such as sheep and cattle live together in large groups. These animals roam across large expanses of farmland, sleeping and eating. Farmers often need to move groups of these animals to different parts of their farms. They rely on the help of dogs to accomplish this. Dogs can lead the groups of **livestock** to wherever the farmers need them to go. Dogs also make sure that stray sheep or cows do not wander away from the group.

Many different dog breeds have been used over the years to **herd** livestock. Each has its own way of working. English sheepdogs round up sheep by simply barking and running around the outside of a group. Rottweilers encourage cattle to move by running into them, while corgis run in between the animals and bite them lightly on the legs. Border collies can herd sheep just by staring at them!

FUN FACT! Some farm dogs like to groom the livestock they are guarding or herding by licking them.

Australian shepherds and other farm breeds often help farmers guard or herd livestock.

CHAPTER 3

Born and Raised

Domestic dogs usually reproduce under the supervision of people called breeders. These experts carefully select which male and female dogs will mate with each other to create puppies. Working dogs are almost always purebred. This means that their parents, grandparents, and great-grandparents all come from the same breed. Dogs of different breeds can also mate and produce offspring. Their puppies are sometimes called mutts or crossbreeds.

Breeders look for strong, healthy dogs to mate with each other. Some breeders own both male and female dogs that they breed together. Others contact fellow breeders and arrange to mate their dogs together. After the two dogs mate, they are separated from each other. It takes about nine weeks after mating for the puppies to be born, though the exact time can vary slightly. A mother dog usually gives birth to a litter of between three and ten puppies. Older mothers generally have smaller litters than younger ones do.

Rhodesian Ridgeback puppies are sometimes trained to become guard dogs or hunting dogs.

Training Time

Working dogs begin their training while they are still puppies. Like all dogs, the first thing they need to learn is how to obey commands from their masters. Commands are often spoken words, such as "sit" or "stay." Some trainers also use whistles that only dogs can hear or small devices that produce clicking sounds.

Once a dog has learned basic obedience commands, it can begin learning the skills it needs to do its job. For example, police dogs practice running up and down stairs and jumping over obstacles. This allows them to chase after fleeing criminals. They are also taken out into public so they can get used to being around large crowds without getting distracted. Guard dogs are taught when they should and shouldn't bark. They also learn not to accept treats from people other than their trainers or masters. This ensures that intruders cannot distract the dogs with food.

Military dogs are trained to perform tasks blindfolded so they can perform missions even when their vision is limited.

Constant Companions

Seeing, hearing, and other assistance dogs need more specialized training than most working dogs. These dogs share unique relationships with their owners. The dogs must learn how to analyze situations and react without commands from their owners. They must recognize when their owners need help and how best to assist them.

Most assistance dogs are bred and trained by organizations that specialize in doing this. After about a year and a half of basic obedience training, they learn how to recognize obstacles or important sounds. They also learn how to lead people and keep a pace that their owners can follow.

Once the dogs have been trained, the organizations match them with people who need them. However, they do not simply hand the dogs over. The dogs and humans must first practice working together under the supervision of an expert trainer. The trainer must approve the pairing before the person is allowed to take the dog home permanently.

Trainers work with assistance dogs and their owners to make sure each dog and person are a good match.

CHAPTER 4

The Dawn of Domestication

Scientists believe that the first dogs appeared on Earth somewhere between 40 million and 30 million years ago. These early dogs were the ancestors of all of today's dogs, wolves, and foxes. Humans eventually began to recognize the strength, intelligence, and sensory abilities of dogs. Scientists have found evidence indicating that humans may have begun keeping domestic wolves more than 16,000 years ago. Many of these early dogs helped people hunt or herd animals. They were also kept as livestock in some places.

As new human civilizations developed over time, dogs became even more closely tied to people. **Archaeologists** have discovered cave paintings throughout the world that depict people interacting with dogs. Many people in ancient Chinese, European, and Middle Eastern societies kept domestic dogs. The ancient Egyptians believed that dogs were sacred. Some Egyptian dogs were even assigned human servants to wait on them.

Ancient rock art found in Libya and other parts of the world show humans interacting with dogs.

Selective Breeding

At some point, people began to realize that some dogs were better suited to certain jobs than others were. Some dogs were natural-born hunters. Others were smaller and less aggressive, making for excellent pets. Early dog breeders found that if they mated two dogs that shared a certain characteristic, the resulting puppies would likely have that characteristic as well. Over the course of many generations, humans used this practice to develop the wide variety of dog breeds that exist today. Some of these breeds have existed in some form for thousands of years, while others were only recognized as distinct breeds in more recent times.

Today, organizations such as the American Kennel Club and the Kennel Club of the United Kingdom keep records of purebred dogs so that breeders can be sure the dogs they mate together are indeed the same breed. This helps ensure that pure breeds do not lose their unique traits by mixing with other kinds of dogs.

Generations of selective breeding have produced dogs
as different as the tiny Chihuahua and the large Great Dane.

CHAPTER 5

Quitting Time

Working dogs lead very different lives from those of everyday pet dogs. But they still require many of the same basic comforts to be happy and healthy. Just like pet dogs, working dogs enjoy socializing with humans and other dogs. They like to play, and they love being rewarded with treats for their hard work.

Just like human workers, dogs eventually reach a time when they should **retire**. Age, injury, or health problems can prevent the dogs from doing their jobs effectively. However, most retired working dogs still have many years left to enjoy their lives. Rescue dogs often retire when they are between eight and ten years old. Assistance dogs also retire when they are around that age. Though assistance dogs form very close bonds with their owners, their unique relationship may not allow the pair to stay together. The dog can no longer care for the person, and the person might be unable to care for the dog.

Most working dogs can be kept as pets once they have retired.

A Happy Home

Some working dogs continue to live with the families of their handlers after retiring. Sometimes, people looking for pets that are already **housebroken** and obedient adopt retired working dogs. To adopt a retired working dog, most organizations require people to fill out applications that determine whether or not they are suited to care for a dog. If approved, the people are placed on a waiting list to receive a dog once one becomes available. This can take anywhere from weeks to years, depending on the organization and the type of dog being adopted.

Some working dogs must go through additional training or screening before they can be adopted. For example, military dogs are often trained to be aggressive toward humans that they view as enemies. As a result, military dog handlers must test the dogs to make sure they will not unexpectedly bite their new owners. Once dogs are ready for adoption, they can go on to lead happy lives with their new families, just as every dog deserves.

Working dog adoption organizations take great care in making sure dogs and their new owners are ready for adoption.

Words to Know

ancestors (AN-ses-turz) — ancient animal species that are related to modern species

archaeologists (ahr-kee-AH-luh-jists) — scientists who study the distant past, often by digging up old artifacts and fossils

bred (BRED) — kept under controlled conditions to produce quality offspring

breeds (BREEDZ) — particular types of a plant or animal

carnivores (KAR-nih-vorz) — animals that have meat as a regular part of their diet

climates (KLYE-mits) — the weather typical of places over a long period of time

domestic (duh-MES-tik) — tamed

handlers (HAND-lurz) — people who command and supervise working dogs

herd (HURD) — to move animals together in a group

housebroken (HOUS-broh-kin) — trained to go to the bathroom outside rather than indoors

instincts (IN-stingkts) — natural behaviors or responses

litter (LIT-ur) — a number of baby animals that are born at the same time to the same mother livestock (LIVE-stahk) — animals that are kept or raised on a farm or ranch

mate (MAYT) — to join together to produce babies

muzzles (MUZ-uhlz) — extended noses and mouths on some animals

peripheral (puh-RIF-ur-uhl) — of or having to do with the outer edge of something

prey (PRAY) — an animal that is hunted by another animal for food

retire (ri-TIRE) — to stop working, usually because of reaching a certain age

sacred (SAY-krid) — very important and deserving great respect

species (SPEE-sheez) — one of the groups into which animals and plants of the same genus are divided

terrain (tuh-RAYN) — an area of land

Habitat Map

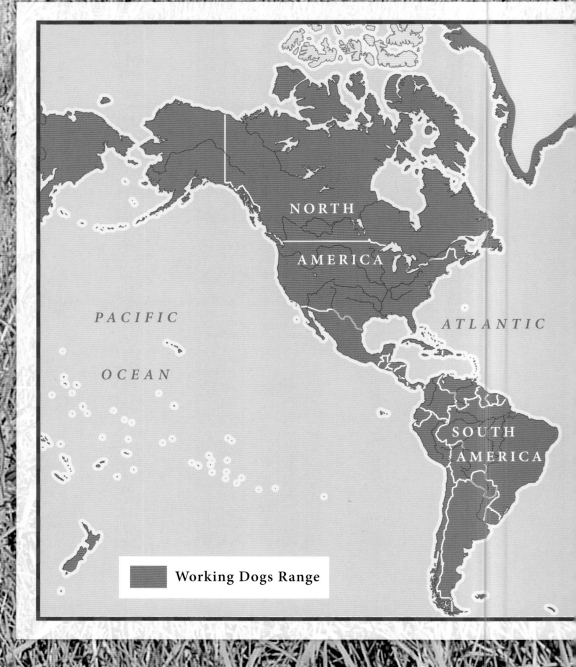

NORTH

AMERICA

PACIFIC

OCEAN

ATLANTIC

SOUTH

AMERICA

Working Dogs Range

ARCTIC OCEAN

ASIA

EUROPE

PACIFIC OCEAN

AFRICA

INDIAN OCEAN

OCEAN

OCEAN

AUSTRALIA

Find Out More

Books

Bozzo, Linda. *Police Dog Heroes*. Berkeley Heights, NJ: Enslow Publishers, 2011.

Gorrell, Gena K. *Working Like a Dog: The Story of Working Dogs Through History*. Plattsburgh, NY: Tundra Books, 2003.

Stamper, Judith Bauer. *Eco Dogs*. New York: Bearport Publishing, 2011.

Visit this Scholastic Web site for more information on working dogs:
www.factsfornow.scholastic.com
Enter the keywords **Working Dogs**